FINDING YOUR COLORS

Spreading the Pollen...

Coloring the World...

All original art by Tetê AmO

Please contact me if you would like more information about my paintings or to share your thoughts.

I would love to hear from you!

©2019 by the author of this book

Tereza Amaral de Oliveira - Tetê AmO

ISBN - 978-1-7329038-1-4

Acknowledgment

I dedicate this book to my heavenly Father,
Who guided me, inspired me, and made it possible!

I am forever thankful to my parents,
Armindo de Oliveira
and Lidia David do Amaral
for teaching me how to keep my colors!
I was blessed with parents
who were true to their colors.
Now, enjoying together heavenly colors!

A special thank you to Sr. Clare Briody for her help, being a sparkle of light and love,
and to all who gave me support offering their prayers.

Grateful for God's little helpers, the bees and the butterflies,
for their great work keeping us alive!

To My Mom with Love

She always knew how to keep her colors bright.
She is now on a journey of purity and peace.
She has flown away, but supernaturally, she is closer than ever because now she is living in my heart, still speaking words of comfort, being present in everything I do, for her wisdom, her beauty, her kindness and cheerful heart will always be remembered.
Now, it is time for her to rest, together with my lovely and unforgettable father.
They were a heavenly match, and I know that now they will be happy forever.
They had missed each other for too long.

Daddy and mom, you are both in my heart and I will love you forever.
Thank you!

My mom, Lidia, passed away on September 1, 2019. She was the first to see this book. When I wrote FINDING YOUR COLORS, I did not know how it would touch people's hearts. Now I know, because it has brought so much joy and truth to mine, in a moment like this.

My parents always knew how "TO BE". They were faithful in every role of their lives and their mission, like the butterflies, that migrate guided by a supernatural power without wavering in the direction of their destiny. Reading this book, you will see three hearts merging, my parents and mine, expressing our love to you!

Sometimes,

to preserve our colors,

we have to help others

to find theirs.

Table of Fun in Colorful Contents

Where Are Your Colors?

Traveling to a Colorful World

Surrounded by Colors

Restoring Your Colors

Fertilizing Colors

Finding Your Colors

Spreading the Pollen

Where Are Your Colors?

The Bee Buzzing Around

I am a pollinator

Time to spread the love!

I feel adventurous today!

I will explore

I will travel far and beyond

I will kiss sweet flowers

They are waiting for me!

I will collect nectar and pollen

I have a lot to do!

Fertilization depends on me!

Making honey is important to me

Wax making takes a lot of energy

I will tremble dance

I will use the waggle dance

For the survival of my colony

I also can sting

I am a little bee!

Don't be afraid!

Your life depends on me!

I can make your life sweet; honey

The world is colorful because of me!

Take good care of me!

Crops are calling!

Come, have fun with me!

The bee:

Wow! What kind of place is this?

Where did the colors go?

I have so much work to do!

A Ray of Light!

In the dark cave, a ray of light, full of energy, comes frantic trying to understand how a place like this could even exist! The bee only understands light and colors. Wherever it goes, it brings life! And this place is in desperate need of hard work!

Sometimes,

A TINY SPARKLE
IS ALL WE NEED

to open our eyes!

For the bee, there is only one thing to be done; restoration!
The bee has a purpose and it will be accomplished!
The butterfly needed a push to find its colors.
The butterfly got so comfortable, that it felt asleep and forgot its purpose.

The halfhearted butterfly:

I think today I will just rest.

I will just go to sleep!

Ouch! That hurts!

The bee said, surprised:

Who are you, as sad as can be?

The butterfly:

Who are you, buzzing around,
as happy as can be?

I am a butterfly, who would you be?

The bee:

I am sorry that I stung you.
I did not recognize you.
I am a bee!
What happened to your colors?

The butterfly:

I think I lost my colors!
I don't know where to find them.

The bee, holding the butterflies' wings:

Would you like me to help you to find them?

The butterfly:

Ah, you are very kind,
but I am too tired!
It is ok, not to have any colors.
Maybe, they will find me!
This place is enough for me!

The bee:

If you come with me,
I will show you something beautiful and delicious.
I will show you who you are supposed to be!
I need your help, and you need me!
You can give joy!
Please, will you just trust me?

The butterfly:

I am only a butterfly!
What can I be?
Look at my size!
Who needs me?

The bee:

For your information, colors depend on you!
To enrich the world, is our job to do!
You will love your new you, and all you can do!

The butterfly:

I will go just for a little while.
Do you, little bee, have a better place for me?
I am holding on to your promises,
so, please, guide me!

Confidence

What is that,

that looks so sad and dull?

Where is the light?

I cannot see!

I look around, but there is nothing to see!

My colors are fading away!

Wait a minute!

Don't take my colors away!

I will share my colors with you!

I will bring light to you!

I'll show you how!

Come, and you will see!

Jump the fence!   Fly away!

New thoughts!   New ways!

You belong where you can say:

"that's it!"

Can you say it today?

The bee has about six weeks to live.

No time to think; "what if?"

It can only "go for it!"

A World to Explore!

The bee took the butterfly to a colorful world, a fountain of nectar. The butterfly, flapping its wings in amazement, smiled and tasted the sweetness of the garden! They played around covering themselves with a yellow powder that made them look funny! They had a great time going from flower to flower, kissing them with promises of sharing their sweetness. Lavender, cosmos, verbena, marigolds, sunflowers, marjoram, foxgloves, dahlias; all welcoming their helpers to spread their beauty all over the world!

Where is your fountain of nectar?
Are you enjoying this colorful world?
Do you enjoy the sweetness of life?
Do you look funny sometimes?
Do you kiss the day promising to spread the joy you have received?
Are you exploring the colors of your heart that make your wings flap?

Have you ever seen the butterflies migrating?

I was surrounded by thousands of butterflies migrating from a faraway land to another. It was a spectacular sight. They always bring so much joy! I wonder what is engraved in them that shows the way and they follow it with such obedience. They are on a mission, and the only way is to go forward! The journey is long. They will reproduce; others will continue their journey, but the joy that they have spread, will last forever! Little creatures, carrying the responsibility of spreading pollen for fertilization, to keep us alive!

How brave they are!
They came to bring a message!
We also can fly!

Stretching love to distant lands will keep the heart warm when life gets cold, and it will refresh the spirit when life gets hot!

What can they see that I can't?

What do they know that I don't?

Who is directing the butterflies? Instinct?
We also have instinct, but we get lost!
Or, maybe not!
Many times, we don't realize that
we are always being guided!
The difference between us and the butterflies, is
that we frequently fight against the power that
wants to move us forward.
When I feel lost, I am close to being found.
That's when I look for answers,
direction and insight!
And I find it!

God built a fence of protection around us
so we don't need to fence our hearts!

Opening our lives to God we live in expansive joy!

Color Vibrancy

How is your life today? Exciting, full of enthusiasm, rich in colors?
Or, maybe, you feel like the butterfly, sleepy and colorless?
Sometimes, we look for big answers and they come as tiny as the bee!
Sometimes, we can only see what we want to see, but the light will open our eyes.

Wherever we are in life, we were sent for a purpose; to use our colors to bring a sparkle of love to the world! Whoever receives it, will pass it on. If you hide the sparkle that has been given to you, you will miss a chance to be the light, and to give light. Finding your colors will give the opportunity to others to find their own. Remember that, when God blesses one, He never stops there! He gave you light! If the speed of light is 299792458m/s, you can travel that fast to touch someone's heart!

Pollen of Joy

IT DEPENDS ON US TO FERTILIZE

sweet aromas & vibrant colors

TO GIVE LIFE A

honey taste!

Carry the pollen of joy wherever you go!

Fertilize love and kindness!

Recognizing the butterfly, the worker bee also recognized its gifts. The bee knew that the butterfly could never lose its inside colors. In the dark we can't see our colors, but they are still there. The bee took the butterfly by the wings! Can you be like the bee?

Our colors were given by God and nothing can take that away!

We don't have wings, but with the grace of God we can soar!

SOMETIMES, WHAT STOPS US FROM MOVING FORWARD, IS TO KNOW THAT WE WILL HAVE TO FACE WHAT IS UNCOMFORTABLE, FIGHT OUR UNPLEASANT THOUGHTS AND STRETCH OUR STIFF WINGS. WHY SETTLE FOR LESS WHEN WE CAN HAVE THE BEST?

Busy Bee

The bee works hard to keep us alive!
Tiny little creature!
Surely, it does not know it is carrying a
miracle every day!
Short, meaningful life,
spreading the best of gifts!
Reproducing scented, colorful flowers,
and producing honey, are a few of those.

In approximately six weeks they make a difference in the world.
What can you do in six weeks to help them?

Week 1 – Say no to herbicides and pesticides, forever!

Week 2 – Keep a bee and butterfly garden.

Week 3 – Buy local & raw honey from your local beekeepers.

Week 4 – Be informed about the bees and get involved!

Week 5 – Buy certified organic cotton. Cotton crops are the most toxic in the world.

Week 6 – Don't be afraid of them, they will not sting you if you stay still.

Are you traveling in the right direction?

I travel to discover new cultures, to enjoy the new.
It is a big surprise! For me, there are many ways to feel the same excitement on a daily basis; *I surprise my routine!*
I know what brings a smile to my face; simple things that are very precious to me. I have many "bees" coming to me, helping me to always believe that we can fly away to distant lands, to color the world! I have to start coloring my own surroundings and heart, to learn how to reach the world! When I feel like my colors are drifting away, tiny blessings can make them become brighter.

I like to spread seeds all over and forget about it. When they sprout, it feels my heart with joy. I send post cards expressing my feelings of that day, and when I receive it, I relive that moment. I hide little notes and chocolate; I offer a five-minute prayer painting, or I just stop to listen to my Father. Those moments are gifts from God saying:

"I am here with you, and I love you!"

And how can you not smile when you receive those gifts?
Sometimes, God surprises me with unexpected gifts, like the dolphins playing in the ocean when I go for a walk on the beach, butterflies migrating, the visit of a single bee, and the high-five of a cheerful kid passing by!
Experiencing the joy that God sends my way, I travel in His word, in His company and He carries me to light.

The bee took the butterfly to light, and they flew away to enjoy plenty of nectar!

Join in this colorful adventure!

Which one is your palette?

One

Two

Three

Four

Five

1 – Color of hope! Blessings indeed! Light and serenity!

2 – A mix of joy, peace, and sweetness, all in harmony!

3 – Uplifting color calming the mind!

4 – Enthusiastic and fun!

5 – Vibrant, energetic and playful!

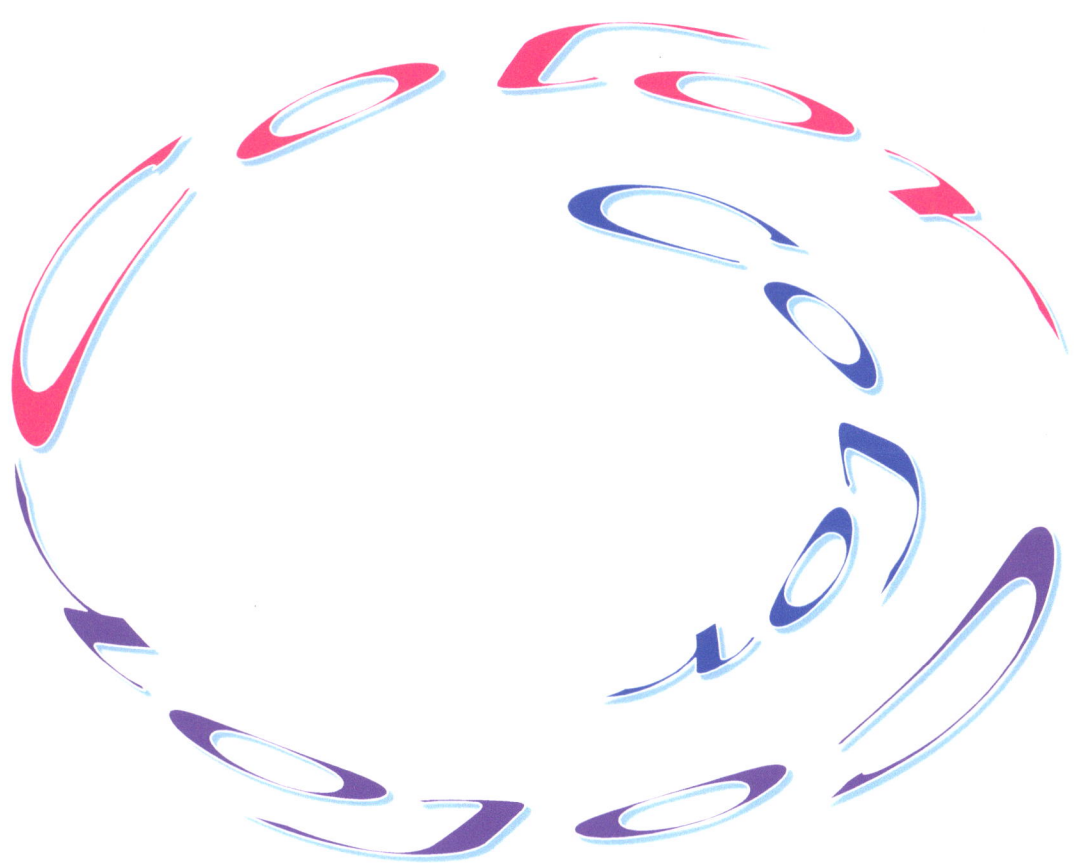

Surrounded By Colors

The bee to the butterfly:

There is something happening to you.

The butterfly:

What is it?

The bee:

I can see some colors in you.

The butterfly:

How can this be?

The Gift

One day, I asked God;
"Is this it?"
He grabbed my hand and said:
"It depends on how you see Me!"

One day, I saw myself as a box covered tightly with a beautiful ribbon;
I asked God:
"What is inside?"
And God said:
"I am"!

One day, I felt that there was more to explore than what I could see;
I asked God:
"What do you see?"
God said:
"A gift from Me!"

One day, I knew that I had to open my heart and let it be!
I asked God:
"How can it be?"
And God answer:
"You just have to trust Me!

And God colored my world with His happy colors!

Surrounded by Pink!

I am definitely a pink girl!

I dressed in pink to celebrate New Year's. More than making resolutions, I wanted to start the year "wearing" my resolution, coloring my heart in pink. I am God's little girl, and I will always be! Being a child in the heart, is the exact place where God wants us to be. A child who trusts in the Majestic power of her Father and keeps going! When I am surrounded by pink flowers, when I wear pink, or decorate my little paradise with pink, I feel exhilarating joy!

Charming, delicate, playful, insightful pink!

A tranquil heart
connected to God
finds peace
and harmony

If you wish, write a few words about how the colors of the painting

on the next page make you feel, before you read the text.

What color is your favorite to have surround you?

Meaningful Colors

Passion and love
are the center of life

Peace and joy surround this intense love

Beauty planted in a broken vase
is illuminated by compassion,
placed on a table of abundant joy,
covered by heavenly Divine protection

With faith, purified and anointed,
the healing power of God is manifested

I walk along the river of truth,
as a daughter, holding
my Father's Majestic hands

Sprinkling passionate praises

Glowing, flourishing, restored

Sharing the light that He pours into me!

Seasonal Colors

My favorite seasons are Spring and Fall. I was born on both seasons, considering that the hemispheres have opposite seasons. I believe that I am very influenced by these renewing seasons, in different ways. I am attracted by the new. Learning something new, exploring new possibilities, letting the seeds that I have planted in my heart take root, and letting go of the old, gives me a boost of energy. I keep going, expecting more revelations each day. New ways of seeing and experiencing life is very exciting! I want to be free to go and find infinite blessings that God sprinkles out there, and I want to enjoy it, as much as I possibly can. They all come in colors!

I feel them, don't you? Simple pleasures in life to explore
I love Spring colors, for it takes me to a place of joy.
The warmth of Fall colors inspires me to new dreams.
Summer colorful umbrellas suggest that it is time to have fun!
In Winter, white snowflakes shower the earth with peace and hope!

We go through seasons;

CHANGING,

RENEWING,

DISCOVERING WAYS

that take us to other seasons with a fresh start.

The beauty of it is that it never gets old,
it is always a surprise!

Get your wings going!

Winter Colors

Where I live, I start the new year in Winter. I think it is perfect to start anything in life with a peaceful heart. Winter is the coziest season. I am happy just lying down on my couch, covered by a soft blanket, reading a book, drinking hot chocolate, adding fairy lights to create an ambience of charm. It is magical! In Winter, I have more time to meditate, to think about what I would like to accomplish that is valuable, and how I can use my happy colors, not only on canvas.

For some, winter is not the most cheerful season, but when we are expecting to find connection with God, I would say, it is the perfect season. It seems that nothing is happening, the colors are fading away,

It is time to connect and cultivate food for the spirit!

nature is sleeping. We feel the same, snugged in our comfortable and warm blanket, waiting for spring. If we could only be in winter; one season at a time, we would recognize that without one season, we would not have the other. Our roots are alive in any season, but we lose our leaves, and we feel cold. Like the bees clustered in winter, we also may spend this time getting our hearts warm. The group hug saves the bees in winter, and we also find healing hugging God's word. He covers us with a blanket of love to gather enough food for all seasons. At this time of the year, the bees are exercising their wing's muscles. They feed on honey, we feed on the sweetness of God's company and word. We are being prepared to sprout! We can't rush, or our branches and buds might not be so luxurious. It is the time when we feed our colors for spring. No matter if we feel unseen, or we want to be unseen, spring will come, and we better be prepared to be seen! That's why we can't rush. That's when we get our strength back to come out of the cocoon!

Spring Colors

I love Spring for it brings me to a place of joy.
I am renewed after hibernating with my
Father, refreshing my spirit with warm
nourishment. I want to squeeze every drop of
joy that this season is offering and collect
nature's happy findings. It is time to see in
display all that I have prepared my heart to
receive. It is time to put into practice the
wisdom received in Winter
and learn with the rebirth of nature!
It is time for action, to come out to the light!
It seems to be a very short season for all the
miracles that are taking place!
The bees and butterflies are ready to work!
How about you?

What comes to mind when you think about Spring?

Everything new! Explosion of colors! Bloom! Renewal! Regrowth!

It is time to pollinate, to renew and bloom new colors!

Bright and new!

We are being renewed by God!
The seeds that you planted in your heart are ready to germinate!

Summer Colors

Vibrant umbrellas are banners announcing: the wait is over!

Time to have fun! We are totally surrounded by colors! Even our skin shows a happy color! It is time for colorful clothes, decorated sandals, and beach towels, all in perfect harmony with the magnificent blue of the water. We have not a care in the world! Our feet are massaged by the sand, we cool ourselves in the water, life is good! Sea gulls invite their guests to play in the water, it is a show of happiness! A season abundant with activities! We have had this feeling every year of our lives. It is a season that brings great teaching. We know for sure that summer will come. We never doubt, we prepare our to do list, expecting what is coming for sure! We make plans, we are out there! Here we go!

Expect it as children, that your Father has prepared
seasons of exhilarating joy!
Colors that will never fade away!

The wait is over!
It is a promise!

Fall Colors

The skies are celebrating this season displaying a glorious canvas every evening from the mighty hand of God! A season of thanksgiving for so much that nature offers and **fall** for it! The colors of fall are stunning, the leaves on the ground speak loudly when we walk on them, saying that even though they have fallen, they will come back. I was passing by maple trees that were already losing their bright colors, turning into a faded brown. I sat down under the tree to paint, covering myself from the bright sunshine coming in my direction. I looked up and I was stunned by what I saw. The leaves were lemon yellow, so gorgeous in contrast with the blue sky, and rays of sunlight sparkling like crystals!

This is what light can do! It intensifies our colors!

We only have to receive it! Sometimes, just seeing it from a different angle, life can have a stunning colorful look!

Peace

No matter which season I am going through, I know it is called a season for a reason! It will keep moving, keep changing me, like the leaves in the fall changing its colors, or the new buds coming alive in Spring! With great expectations to see the outcome, I focus on learning from it, having a deeper connection with God. When we find peace in every season, we master our emotions with joy!

God
beckons you
to experience
joy & peace!

I went to visit Death Valley to see the wild flowers. I was very impressed to see miles and miles of flowers, it is such a spectacular sight! Even though it was winter, it was hot. I spent the night in Bishop, a delightful town, and I went for a day trip to Mammoth. I had a little bit of all seasons in one weekend. Spring flowers, Summer heat, yellow Fall colors, and Winter freezing cold!

But I was prepared!

Going through different seasons in life, we get stronger and more confident, for each one brings a new teaching. Instead of hiding in the cave, losing our colors, there is a better refuge where to hide: under God's wings. There, we will be fine for all seasons!

Winter Peace – Spring New

Summer Promises

Fall Thanksgiving

RESTORING

YOUR

COLORS

The butterfly to the bee:

I know what is happening little bee!
It is coming back to me!
My colors are showing,
who I might be!

The bee:

You sure look different,
it is good to see!
You are fluttering away,
just wait for me!

The butterfly to the bee:

Hurry up, little bee!
There is much to see!
I was in the dark but now I can see!

Heavenly Identity

What is your heavenly Father's name?

What is your name?

What is the name that God has given you?

New Name

We gave been given a name, but only God can give us a significant name that shows our uniqueness, as He has done changing a person's name in the Bible. It is God's desire to change us until we fit in our real name that make us distinct from others. Our heavenly name tells a story about the specific assignment God has prepared for each one of us.

Think about how God is unlimited in everything He does, and He has created.

We might have similar gifts but the name that God inscribed on those gifts cannot be altered.

God created a colorful world and you are His primary color!

Please, remember that when life tries to take your colors away!

Metamorphosis

From an egg, to be able to fly, the butterfly goes through a process of development that is natural, beneficial, and necessary. From the first moment of being an egg, it goes through a challenge for a month. An egg turns into chrysalis, then reaches adult life, ready to fly!

It sheds its skin, hang upside down, turn into a mummy, taking their time to strength their wings, getting ready for freedom!
I see every step as a miracle. Finally, the butterfly comes to light; gorgeous, and with a mission! It would be indeed unfortunate to have this miracle stop there, for the butterfly could lose its colors, its identity.

All is planned by God's hand! The process of developing spiritual growth, confidence, finding purpose and meaning, also takes time and patience. We come to light after nine months, upside down. We take some time to stand up, and we still need to be transformed from the inside, which takes a life time! Again, we can't rush the process, but we can help ourselves, getting help from God. Before we open our wings, we have to open our hearts to Him!

Then, you will be confident to soar wearing your colors!

Precious

Can you see your true colors?

If you only could see yourself through God's eyes

You would see that He painted your heart with everlasting colors

With love that cannot be changed by life's circumstances

You would see a masterpiece

Would you wake up singing?

Would you go through the day dancing?

Would you flutter your wings with joy?

Would your true colors give you butterflies?

Would you recognize yourself?

How would your life be?

Light

Sunflowers face the sun, for the warmth attracts pollinators and produces better growth. Their leaves track the sun for photosynthesis, to generate oxygen. There are many things involved in this process. I am fascinated by the complexity of nature. It all looks like magic! Plant the seed, add a little water, and voilà! Walking through a sunflower field is all about pleasing the eyes with shimmering sunflowers, radiant and tall greeting their visitors. A display of grandiosity! It is all written in their identity! Their purpose, height, colors, and geometric pattern of the seeds multiplying their beauty.

We are complex beings with an identity that cannot be rewritten!

The sunflower will never lose its color, as long as it can be in the light!

Coloring Your Thoughts

Meditating on God's word
is the best way
to control my thoughts.
There is nothing
more inspiring to me!
But I also like to play a game
painting my thoughts with

bright,

happy,

comforting,

healing

and joyful colors!
It works for me!

Harmonious thoughts make
room for inspiration and clarity.

As I fly away, collecting pollen of beauty, with the movement of my wings, I shake off all that can take my colors away so I can get more pollen to go on my way!

Bee Amazing!

I am in love with bees and butterflies!

I have one lavender plant and a bee that comes to visit me. I write thinking about my little friend. I used to run away when I saw a bee. At the lavender field, they have a very uplifting beat going on, buzzing and dancing to the rhythm of their own symphony! Maybe, inebriated by the sweet aroma of lavender, I was not afraid! I was elated! When I think about a bee stinging me, my heart breaks, for I know that it will be the end for such an amazing little creature that can only do good for all of us!

Would you plant a little paradise for the bees and butterflies, today?

Be the "Bee"

Have you ever had a "bee" coming to your life when you needed a boost of confidence? I believe that we all have! But sometimes, we need more than that. We need restoration from inside; a Guide! Literally, we want someone to take us by the wing to be able to fly! It would be great if we could just handle whatever we don't want to deal with, to the hands of God, and have the solution first thing in the morning; ready to follow instructions and move on!

Well, good news! We can!

It is the only way we can really overcome anything in life! But the way it happens is not so simple. We go through a process of mutation to be able to understand the instructions, then we see the outcome flourishing. Being the "bee" to someone helps us go through this process to fly higher, learning, and holding onto each other's wings!

And God holds us all!

Tenderness

Answers come to us when

we get our minds out of

ourselves, concentrating on

the majestic power of

God

finding refuge in

His

word, and trusting in

Him

Fertilize your soul for a stunning blooming season

Pollen of Joy!

The bee and the butterfly are attracted to the pollen, nectar and the scent of the flowers.

The pollinators benefit from the nectar and pollen of the flowers

The flowers reproduce via pollination

We benefit from this perfect arrangement!

We are attracted to kindness, love,

and anything that brings us joy.

A smile, cheerful words or thoughtful wishes.

Pollinators carry the pollen to the next flower

We carry the love

They need the nectar from the flowers

We need love

We reproduce love by giving it!

Every time we receive it, we pass it on!

Carry the pollen of joy wherever you go!

Fertilize compassion and goodness!

A Sweet Bouquet

I am always finding new herbs growing from seeds that
I have planted randomly mixed with my geraniums.

They are **seeds of joy!**
I don't want to write down what I have sown,
just for fun!
I love surprises!
I buy flowers with closed buds and I keep picking on
them to see what color will be revealed!

Every day we have an opportunity to make life
a little bit more special and fun!

Every smile works as fertilizer to our spirit!

A bouquet of flowers is a unique gift, each one prepared
with a touch of love and creativity,
with aroma of happiness!
Colorful ribbons hold a display of the gentleness of God!
Never let go of those precious moments! They are simple things that work as an ointment restoring us.
Every time our hearts rejoice, it is a prayer of thanksgiving!
A blessing of healing and comfort!

Optimum Growth

For our plants to grow, we need to keep fertilizing the soil, and we also need the pollinators, the bees and butterflies for fertilization. The fertilizer replenishes lost nutrients in the soil and pollination is necessary for many plants to reproduce. The pollinators also benefit receiving nectar from flowers. They are vital for our food supply. We depend on them to survive!

With nature we learn a lot about how to obtain optimum growth through healthy diet and lifestyle. We also need to replenish nutrients in our bodies, a healthy environment, and food for the spirit to keep strong with deeper roots, to stand tall like the palm tree that bends over, but does not break.

A Little Show

One ordinary day
Butterflies came to visit me
They were everywhere
Flying around me
I wanted to hear the message
But it was so clear
I needed no sound
In silence they came to greet me
A message they showered over me
Looking at them I could hear the voice of God
"Trust Me!
I brought you here
Can you see that I planned this special moment
just for you?
Can you understand My power
of orchestrating this moment?
Can you feel My presence?
Many gifts I gave to you
Many more I have for you
They will burst into bloom like the crocus
Just come and see

You think you are waiting
But they are already here
Can you see?
I Am here!
You walk in faith
I will take you there as I brought you here
I will send My angels to fly around you
Blessing the desires that I put in your heart
Manifesting all of them to answer your prayers
You will soar as a young girl
You will see my hands making you bloom
This joy that you feel will be magnified!
The talents and gifts will be amplified!
Trust Me!
Your heart is so grateful for such small things
Much more and bigger I have to bring
My promises to you I will never forget
Moments like this for us to dance and sing
My daughter I love you
I want you to know,
these butterflies I sent you,
are just a little show!"

Promises

The grace of God is infinite, always restoring and multiplying blessings.

Creation shows us a glimpse of His light and promises. From one seed, we get several fruits. Everything is renewed at His time. Planting, fertilizing, pruning, and harvesting can't be rushed! We also grow, we are renewed, restored and blessed with fruits to enjoy. Everything is transformed, nothing is lost! The rain turns brown hills into lush greenery. We might feel that some dreams got lost somewhere in time, but every promise will never be forgotten. Sometimes, our dreams just need to be fertilized, and everything will come back to us at His timing, in double measure!

I AM FED BY THE ABUNDANCE THAT
NATURE FREELY GRANTS ME.
I AM HEALED BY GOD'S TOUCH
RENEWING MY SPIRIT.
I AM SURROUNDED BY
PEACE AND TRANQUILITY.
LISTENING TO A DEEPER SONG
THAT GUIDES ME EVERY DAY.

IN SILENCE I FIND *abundant insight*

IN REST I FIND *serenity*

IN STILLNESS I FIND *answers*

LOOKING UP I FIND *Divine joy!*

The butterfly:

You look funny, little bee!

The bee:
Why? What do you see?

The butterfly:
You are smeared with yellow stuff!

The bee:
You look silly, just like me!

The butterfly:
How sweet life can be!
Thanks to you, my honey bee!

Swimming in the

Living Water

of

Divine Grace!

The bee:

OMG! Who would you be?

The Butterfly:

Don't play with me!

This is the new me!

The bee:

I love your colors!

Fancy indeed!

You look just like a rainbow

With two glowing wings!

The butterfly:

I'm dressed in all colors

That you have shown me!

Now, I am protected

You won't sting me!

I feel like dancing!

Now, come with me!

The bee:

We drink a sweet nectar

How lucky are we!

Dancing and kissing

The flowers to be!

Iridescent

Butterflies can blend in with the environment, as well as a variety of other animals, for protection. It is called camouflage. They only temporarily change their colors; they don't lose their colors!

Sometimes, we compromise because we think we are protecting ourselves, but we are just losing our true self. Instead of losing our colors, it would be more rewarding if we could transform the environment with our colors. Many animals are colored by what they eat, like the flamingos. We also need to absorb light to be able to reflect light.

.

Be Iridescent!

Special, in intense brilliant colors, painting the hearts around you
with the Light of the world!

I learn how to trust
To calm down my heart
I have all it takes!
I have God!
Shine for God!
Even if no one sees it
He is the love of your life
You are His star
Shine for God!
And, what else really matters?

Watching the sunrise
I learn how to approach life

Rising in slow motion
Expanding horizons
Gentle movement
Allowing the dreams to wake up inside my quiet heart
In peace, there is a conversation without words
I receive the light that comes as a gentle caress,
but it is burning with a flame of intense love
It sings a song that will accompany me all day long
Carrying away emotions, thoughts, desires to God,
to bring back, answers, healing, hope,
and new opportunities
Faith is empowering my spirit

Scintillating

If we could see colors with more intensity

With the eyes of a DRAGONFLY

We would be chasing them all

Collecting them

Sharing them

We would be immersing in them

If we could produce our own light like the FIREFLY

Light would be everywhere

Touching

Healing

Loving

If we could shine when disturbed like the NOCTILUCA
There would be more joy
The world would be scintillating
Amazing to see

But we are only humans, what do we do?
We ask the Creator, to shine like they do!

We have a gift for you!

Flowers carrying sweet words, written with honey!

Love

Joy

Harmony

Ligth

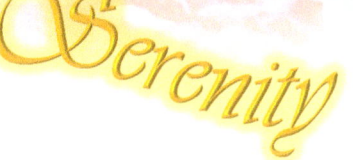

Strength

Serenity

The Rainbow Eucalyptus

It sheds the bark showing its colors.

To reveal our colors to the world,
we need to shed some bark!

There are many colors to show!
What do you need to shed?

What is the size of your dream?

I noticed that some things that happened in my life were not even in my dreams,
but they fit perfectly to take me to my dreams.

Sometimes, we outgrow our dreams.
The desires that we had once, if it had happened,
would have stopped us from reaching bigger dreams!

Today, I am coloring the world!

Pink Dreams

Colors have a surprising way of evoking emotions.
When we are secure of who we are, we are confident to wear
our colors, we can be bold to choose from vibrant to soothing
and let them bring out the best we have to offer.
Colors really have an effect on me!
Yellow sunflower for a touch of the sun inside the house, red
roses to spark the love, lavender to sooth the soul, so delicate,
announcing spring! Each one unique in their gift!
Blue is serene. The blue sky reflected on water invites us to
connect and relax! So refreshing, so inspiring!
It represents holiness.
A touch of magenta and teal is like looking to a huge cascading
ice cream sundae; same feeling!
Green for me is the color of sanity! I need to be walking in
green pastures, literally!
Orange brings out my playful mode and impulsive reactions!
I love pink and white for anything!
White is always a sign of peace! It makes me think about
grace, new beginnings with pure joy!
Pink is for me! It is a combination of all my favourite feelings!
Sweet, tender and charming, it is also the color of sensitivity.

I want to soak in pink bubbles, eating pink rose macarons, drinking rose champagne,
light aromatic rose candles and have pink dreams!

Fabulous pink!

A note for you!

Dear friend,

I want you to know that I got my colors back! I was inside this cave, but I did not know there was a better place for me. Then something stung me! I was awakened by a little bee! It grabbed my wings to go to places to which I did not want to go. I told the bee to leave me alone, but it did not listen to me! That little bee has so much energy! But little by little, the bee took me to taste something so sweet that I wanted some more. It was colorful and fun! We played some games to see who would kiss more flowers. The bee asked me if I was getting tired. No, I said! I want to flutter away and play with you! So, after many kisses, the bee told me that I was getting my colors back. I could feel my wings stronger and faster. Now, I got my colors back, and we have a lot of work to do! Don't think it is the end, we just started, you will see!

I got a new friend, new colors, and a new life! I love the little bee! I thank my friend for stinging me or I would be sleeping my life away. The little bee works so hard but doesn't know what else to do! My friend is a bee, what can I say?

I am a butterfly, and everybody needs me! You will hear me singing when I pass by!

To all who need to find their colors, I hope my story will help you to see, that you are special, and fun you can be! Always remember to whom you belong, there is a ray of Light always waiting for you! You have all that is required to fly high; you don't need wings; He will show you how to fly!

So long my friend, I have to go, there are a lot more flowers to kiss and I want to win this game!

Kisses from a colorful butterfly!

Grace takes us to new adventures into a rainbow of colors. Like the butterflies, we have to take the chance and go to places that we have never dreamt of, but when we get there, we fall in love! We recognize in our hearts that it was meant to be!

Grace opens the way, calling us to receive gifts that are bigger than our imagination can reach. We go through a mysterious path, not seeing everything at once, just feeling the flow. Like a flower, it will open up and colors will explode into bloom!

Artwork

Who
else
can
they
be?

They are
equipped
to work,
and so
are we!

How can you create an exquisite masterpiece?
If we could ask this question of the bee and butterfly, the answer would be:

Be yourself!

But, be yourself with a purpose, to create, to prosper, to build,
to be in God's showroom, working on your mission!
Then, you can be yourself, with great satisfaction!

Spreading the Pollen. . .

Coloring The World. . .

Precious

God created colors to show us His Magnificent creativity!
We are totally surrounded by colors.
We are living in this never-ending colorful canvas, His work of art!
Colors have an effect on us, and our favorite colors,
tell a little bit about our personality.
I show on my paintings the colors from my heart, telling a little about myself. It has
helped me to see the truth about my heart's colors and know how precious I am,
because I was created by a Master!
We are healed when we can see the truth, and free to be vibrant in His painting. His
precious colors can be shown through us! We are His brush strokes developing a
story never told before! We are too precious to God,
and God is too precious to us to let life take our colors away!

The bee:

Now that we had some fun,

there is one more place to go!

For sure it needs some colors

Are you ready? Let's go?

The butterfly:

My little friend, I trust you

You took me all over the world!

You lead the way, I'll follow

I am more than ready, let's go!

Through the Eyes of a Child

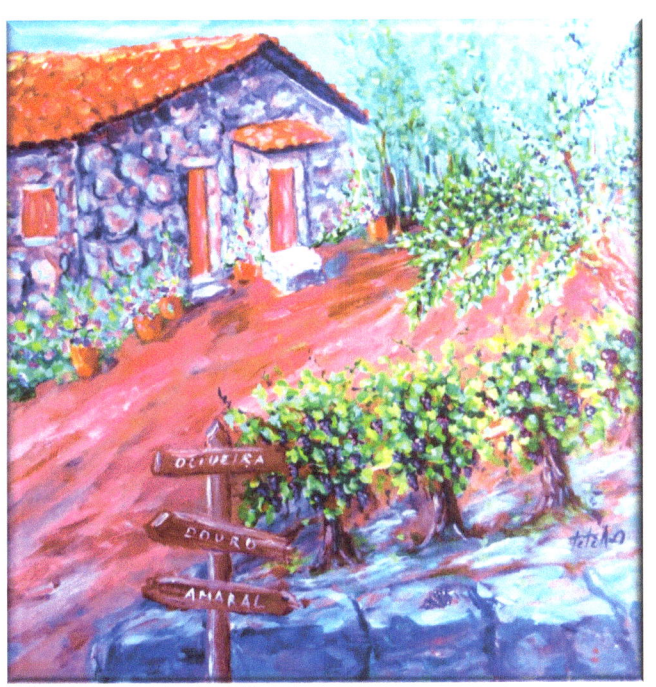

With the eyes of a child, I could picture
the villages where my parents were born.
I kept in my artist heart, Fascinating and
colorful stories with a desire of painting many
places and gardens. Always dreaming!
When I paint, I am free to experiment,
to go wherever it takes me.
My heart is guided by God!
His style is infinite!

Where my colors shine!

Oliveira is my father's last name. Amaral is my mother's last name. Douro is one of the most fantastic places
I have seen. Hills of Divine grape vines as jewels of blessings showing how vast is the goodness of the Lord.
This place has been in my dreams all my life and in some way,
I have lived there, where my roots are, and where my heart belongs!
A place where the stars shine with great intensity and the sun make my colors brighter!

I am going to paint you!

Which butterfly do you choose to flutter your way?

I am splashing colors of
joy over you!
Serenity blue,
lovely pink,
sunny yellow,
and joyful lavander,
twinkling your day!

I chose happy colors
for you, to delight
your day! Enjoy my
visit in this cheerful
garden and share
this feeling today!

Dazziling in
scintillating colors is
what I have for you
today! I will kiss you
and you will shine, to
spread the joy
on your way!

KEEPING MY COLORS

I DECORATE MY QUIET CORNER WITH LIGHT PINK FLOWERS FOR INSTANT TRANQUILITY, SUNFLOWERS TO SPICE THE ATMOSPHERE, AND OTHER FUN SURPRISES THAT I BRING FROM THE FARMER'S MARKET, TO BE INSPIRED BY THEIR BEAUTY! ALMOST EVERYTHING IN MY SANCTUARY IS WHITE TO GIVE IT A CLEAN, PEACEFUL LOOK. I HAVE LAVENDER IN MY BEDROOM NEAR MY BED, FOR SWEET DREAMS, GREENERY ALL OVER TO CAPTURE THE REFRESHING OUTDOOR FEELING AND, OF COURSE, MY LOVELY GERANIUMS DISPLAYING ALL COLORS, SATISFYING THE DESIRES OF THE DAY. IN MY LIVING ROOM I HAVE A HUGE WINDOW AND DOOR WITH A VIEW OF THE GARDEN. I PAINT AT THE SOUND OF THE WATERFALL SURROUNDED BY HUMMINGBIRDS, CONSTANTLY DISTRACTED BY PLAYFUL SQUIRRELS. THE PURPLE DELIGHT OF THE JACARANDA, GORGEOUS PINE TREES, AND HYDRANGEAS, MAKE IT AN ENCHANTED SCENERY. SO MUCH TO CONTEMPLATE! THIS AND MUCH MORE IS AVAILABLE TO ME, EVERY DAY! IT KEEPS ME IN A STATE OF GRATITUDE, ACTIVATING MY COLORS! SIMPLE THINGS HELPING ME TO HAVE A SOFT HEART, APPRECIATING THE UNLIMITED GIFTS OF GRACE, ENCOUNTERING **DIVINE LOVE.**

The bee:

We are carrying the pollen of gratitude today!
It's going to be fun,
to transform the hideaway!

The butterfly:

We will bring some color,
it will shine like the day!
We will spread the pollen,
it will never be the same!

Giving Back with Gratitude

Giving is an act of gratitude.

Watching the wild and fun behavior of the bees and butterflies, I see their excitement going fast from one flower to the other collecting on their bodies, as much pollen as they can. It is an exchange of gifts between them and the flowers. Everything in life is intertwined in this tapestry of giving and receiving.

There are so many gratifying ways to give. We give gifts to someone we love; we give to charity, we give back to the community, and we also should give back to the earth, protecting the fauna and flora. The bees and butterflies do so much for us, we truly depend on them to survive!

We bless and we are blessed, either giving or receiving. When we give, we bless, but we are also blessed, when we give from the heart. Giving involves a thought, a wish of happiness to someone, to show appreciation and love, or it is just an empty box, unexpressed and worthless no matter how much it cost!

The bees and butterflies spread life wherever they go, that's their mission!

We benefit from their hard work.

Let's be good to these powerful, tiny gifts that God gave to us!

Interior Design

I love to decorate everything! It is another way to use my creativity and be surrounded by beauty, reminding me that anything can be transformed to be better. A calming atmosphere invites God to enter. Peace and tranquility are essentials to the heart and mind to connect and listen to the Divine soft voice guiding us. Create a home of hospitality, to celebrate and make memories, to be open to loved ones! Invite nature to come inside! Like the hummingbirds, that right now, are my company as I write, and my little friend, the bee, that comes and goes as it pleases itself and me! Design a place to bless and be blessed!
I have had some friends coming to my place to have a break because here they found serenity.

The best gift we give is to share our colors with love!

First step for a successful home decor is to decorate our hearts with lots of light and colors!
Your heart will show through everything you do! My favorite way to decorate, is to find meaningful memories to add to it and findings that go well with my personality.

Nothing really matches but makes a perfect display Of my interior design!

Mission Accomplished!

The party just started!
The bee and the butterfly invited their friends, the fireflies, to share their light!
All is well, bright and colorful!

Call the fireflies!
Light the candles of hope to welcome the Light of the world!
It comes as a shooting star invading all corners of your life!
His dominant passion reveals His compassion
Indulge, overindulge, treat yourself, relish in this fountain of life!

See you around!

We
will
always
have
extra
pollen
to
cheer
you
up!

Dear friends!
Welcome to these pages of delight! A colorful paradise!
I had a lot of fun flying away with the bees and butterflies!
I hope you had too!

Finding Your Colors, was a gift to me from God

when I asked a simple question: Is this it?

The answer is in every page of this book! But it also made
me realize how insensitive of me to ask God such a question!
He did not mind! He had an impeccable answer for me,
because He is all loving and patient. It is wise to wait on
the Lord for everything, but being still does not mean being
inactive, or "out of service". We should expect great things from
a Magnificent God because He is what He says He is, and He does what He says He does, but some
things are totally up to us. Like getting closer to Him, listening to Him, and be willing to change! The answer to my
question was: "You are losing your colors". Being a lover of colors, the message was very clear! That's Who He
is! He could have given me the most spectacular speech, but He is God! In the Bible, we have the complete speech
of His love for us, but He chose to let me see my heart instead.

After all, He sent salvation using just one Word: Jesus!
Praise God!

I hope this book has inspired you to recognize that all the answers are in your heart!

A pleasure to meet you!

My name is Tereza Amaral de Oliveira, Tetê is my nickname. Tetê AmO Art or Tetê Loves Art, in English, was always in me, but for so long, I could not see it. "AmO" is a combination of the first two letters of my mother's last name "Am" and the initial of my father's last name "O." The three letters together form the word "AmO", which means love, in English.

Following the Light, I am living the dream!

My inspiration comes from the word of God in the Bible. I am also inspired by the creativity of God through nature, communicating with us, teaching and blessing us. My heart delights in God's palette. My books are an expression of my passions as a Christian, a biologist, artist and writer. All my paintings have a special meaning. Some are memories that I want to keep alive, some bring surprises that I can only see after I am finished painting. These are prayerful healing moments guiding me to learn more about myself using my gifts for God's purpose, in ways beyond what I could never have imagined! My books have the purpose to write about what I have learned walking with God, color the world with happy colors, inspire others, and give Him glory!

MORE JOYFUL PAINTINGS
AND WORDS OF ENCOURAGEMENT FOR YOU!

A BOOK TO KEEP IN YOUR HEART!

WHEN YOU OPEN THE WAY TO FREEDOM, YOU ENTER INTO A PRIVATE WORLD OF COLORS AND GENTLE WORDS TO CARESS YOUR HEART! IT IS A BOOK OF ENCOURAGEMENT AND INSPIRATION, AS WELL AS PLEASING TO THE EYES. COLORFUL, CHARMING AND POETIC, IT CHALLENGES YOUR IMAGINATION AND CREATIVITY TO REACH INDIVIDUAL FULFILLMENT. FIND BLISS IN EVERY PAGE, BE TRANSPORTED TO A GARDEN OF JOY! IT IS A MOTIVATIONAL BOOK WITH ART AND REFLECTIONS FOR MEDITATION AWAKENING YOUR DREAMS!

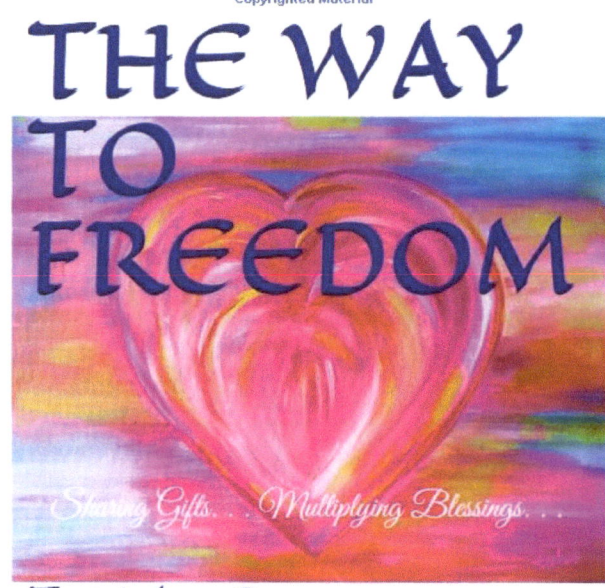

DISCOVER THE TREASURES HIDDEN IN YOUR HEART!
ORIGINAL ART BY TETÊ AMO.

AVAILABLE ON AMAZON.COM

About <u>THE WAY TO FREEDOM</u> by Tetê AmO

A beautiful note from May Kenedy to her friend K. M. about THE WAY TO FREEDOM, that she received as a gift. It touched my heart the way she could capture and describe exactly how the process of writing happens, even though she does not know me personally.

"Dear K. M.,

Wherever did you find such an unusual book?

The art work is stunning. The author/artist <u>looks</u> at something until she really <u>sees</u> it. Then her thoughts just spill out. Most interesting." Mary K.

Alii's Musings
<u>A Beautiful Contemplation of art and reflections</u>
January 7, 2019

Few books have I read that combines the artist's meaning of life shared through her art and creative writing. I am touched by the fundamental insights coming from the sincerity of her heart and faith in God. Through her daily appreciation for the beauties of creation expressed in her artistic creativity and writing, the author invites all readers to discover their dreams, freedom and love for all that they are called to be. Finally, she shares the source of her love for life by the inspiration of her parents and extended family as seen in her paintings and poetic elucidations. This is the first of the author's paperbacks for prayerful reflection and discovering universal freedom through one's heart.

Leone
<u>This book of art and prayer are an inspiration to us all.</u>
February 9, 2019

The beauty and simplicity of this little book inspire me to look at the beauty around me and to see God's creation as I've never seen it before. My prayer life is enriched by Tereza's vision and expression of life, light, color and love of nature. Her words match her art in such a way that you don't know which was created first - or did they both spring together from the loving touch of our Creator? Whatever way it happens, I am looking forward to more of her words and art.

Thank you all for the feedback about how my book touched your hearts,
some showing emotion with tears of joy!
Praise God for using me as an instrument of His love to bless you!

I would love to hear from you!

 Thank you!

 teteamoart@wix.com

 teteamo1@gmail.com

 tete_amo_art

 Tete AmO Art